Under the Sea
Eels

by Jody Sullivan Rake

Consulting Editor: Gail Saunders-Smith, PhD

Consultant: Debbie Nuzzolo
Education Manager
SeaWorld, San Diego, California

Capstone
press

Mankato, Minnesota

Pebble Plus is published by Capstone Press,
151 Good Counsel Drive, P.O. Box 669, Mankato, Minnesota 56002.
www.capstonepress.com

1 2 3 4 5 6 11 10 09 08 07 06

Library of Congress Cataloging-in-Publication Data
Rake, Jody Sullivan.
     Eels / Jody Sullivan Rake.
        p. cm.—(Pebble plus. Under the sea)
     Summary: "Simple text and photographs present the lives of eels"—Provided by publisher.
     Includes bibliographical references and index.
     ISBN-13: 978-0-7368-6362-9 (hardcover)
     ISBN-10: 0-7368-6362-1 (hardcover)
     1. Eels—Juvenile literature. I. Title. II. Series: Under the sea (Mankato, Minn.)
QL637.9.A5R35 2007
597'.43—dc22   2006005051

Editorial Credits
Mari Schuh, editor; Juliette Peters, set designer; Patrick D. Dentinger, book designer; Kelly Garvin,
     photo researcher

Photo Credits
Jeff Rotman, 19; Avi Klapfer, 1
Minden Pictures/Fred Bavendam, cover, 16–17
PhotoDisc Inc., back cover
Seapics/David B. Fleetham, 6–7, 13; Doug Perrine, 5, 11; Masa Ushioda, 20–21
Tom Stack & Associates Inc./Dave B. Fleetham, 9, 14–15

Note to Parents and Teachers

The Under the Sea set supports national science standards related to the diversity
and unity of life. This book describes and illustrates eels that live in seas and oceans.
The images support early readers in understanding the text. The repetition of words
and phrases helps early readers learn new words. This book also introduces early
readers to subject-specific vocabulary words, which are defined in the Glossary section.
Early readers may need assistance to read some words and to use the Table of Contents,
Glossary, Read More, Internet Sites, and Index sections of the book.

Table of Contents

What Are Eels?

Eels are fish

that look like snakes.

Eels have long bodies.

Most are as long

as a baseball bat.

Some are as long as a car.

Some eels are bright colors.

Other eels are dull brown
and dark yellow.

Body Parts

Eels have gills

to help them breathe.

Eels also breathe

through their skin.

gill

Eels have big mouths.

Eels open and close

their mouths again and again

to help them breathe.

What Eels Do

Eels grab prey
with their sharp teeth.
They eat small fish
and shellfish.

Eels swim at night.

They wriggle their bodies

to swim.

Eels rest during the day.
They hide in holes
and cracks in rocks.

Under the Sea

Eels live in warm waters
under the sea.

Glossary

gills—body parts of a fish that help it breathe

prey—an animal hunted by another animal for food

shellfish—an ocean animal kept safe by a shell; clams, oysters, crabs, and snails are shellfish.

wriggle—to move by wiggling back and forth

Read More

Murray, Peter. *Fish.* Science around Us. Chanhassen, Minn.: Child's World, 2005.

Stone, Lynn M. *Eels.* Marine Life. Vero Beach, Fla.: Rouke, 2006.

Woodward, John. *Eels.* Nature's Children. Danbury, Conn.: Grolier, 2004.

Internet Sites

FactHound offers a safe, fun way to find Internet sites related to this book. All of the sites on FactHound have been researched by our staff.

Here's how:

1. Visit *www.facthound.com*

2. Choose your grade level.

3. Type in this book ID **0736863621** for age-appropriate sites. You may also browse subjects by clicking on letters, or by clicking on pictures and words.

4. Click on the **Fetch It** button.

FactHound will fetch the best sites for you!

Index

Word Count: 113
Grade: 1
Early-Intervention Level: 12